WORLD OF WORK

GOVERNMENT

Exploring Career Pathways

Diane Lindsey Reeves

Created and produced by
Bright Futures Press, Cary, North Carolina
www.brightfuturespress.com

Published by
Cherry Lake Publishing, Ann Arbor, Michigan
www.cherrylakepublishing.com

Photo Credits: Cover, Beautyline; page 7, legenda, Peshkova, PRPStudio, everything possible, Photographee.eu, BPTU, Pressmaker, RDaniel; page 8, legenda; page 10, Peshkova; page 12, PRPStudio; page 14, everything possible; page 16, lazyllama; page 18, BPTU; page 20, Pressmaker; page 22, RDaniel; page 24, Eugenio Marongiu.

Library of Congress Cataloging-in-Publication Date

CIP data has been filed and is available at catalog.loc.gov.

Printed in the United States of America.

TABLE OF CONTENTS

Hello, World of Work 4

Take a Hike 6

WoW Up Close 7

- Building Inspector 8
- City Manager 10
- First Responder 12
- Intelligence Analyst 14
- Legislator 16
- Military Serviceperson 18
- Scientist 20
- Special Agent 22

WoW Big List 24

Take Your Pick 26

Explore Some More 27

My WoW 30

Glossary 31

Index 32

HELLO WORLD OF WORK

This is you.

Right now, your job is to go to school and learn all you can.

This is the world of work.

It's where people earn a living, find purpose in their lives, and make the world a better place.

Sooner or later, you'll have to find your way from

HERE to THERE.

To get started, take all the jobs in the incredibly enormous world of work and organize them into an imaginary pile. It's a big pile, isn't it? It would be pretty tricky to find the perfect job for you among so many options.

No worries!

Some very smart career experts have made it easier to figure out. They sorted jobs and industries into groups by the types of skills and products they share. These groups are called career clusters. They provide pathways that will make it easier for you to find career options that match your interests.

- Architecture & Construction
- Arts & Communication
- Business & Administration
- Education & Training
- Finance
- Food & Natural Resources
- Government
- Health Sciences
- Hospitality & Tourism
- Human Services
- Information Technology
- Law & Public Safety
- Manufacturing
- Marketing, Sales & Service
- Science, Technology, Engineering & Mathematics (STEM)
- Transportation

Good thing you are still a kid.

You have lots of time to explore ideas and imagine yourself doing all kinds of amazing things. The **World of Work** (WoW for short) series of books will help you get started.

TAKE A HIKE!

There are 16 career pathways waiting for you to explore. The only question is: Which one should you explore first?

Is **Government** a good path for you to start exploring career ideas? There is a lot to like about this pathway. These professionals run our cities, counties, states, and country. They take care of everything from water supplies and public education to highways and the military.

See if any of the following questions grab your interest.

WOULD YOU ENJOY reading about U.S. presidents, running for student council, or helping a favorite candidate win an election?

CAN YOU IMAGINE someday working at a chamber of commerce, government agency, or law firm?

ARE YOU CURIOUS about what mayors, customs agents, federal special agents, intelligence analysts, or politicians do?

If so, it's time to take a hike! Keep reading to see what kinds of opportunities you can discover along the Government pathway.

But wait!

What if you don't think you'll like this pathway?

You have two choices.

You could keep reading, to find out more than you already know. You might be surprised to learn how many amazing careers you'll find along this path.

OR

Turn to page 27 to get ideas about other WoW pathways.

WoW Up Close

They make our laws and enforce them. They protect us, rescue us, and fight for us. They run the programs, agencies, and departments that keep our cities, states, and nation running smoothly. These are just some of the important jobs that people who work along the Government pathway do.

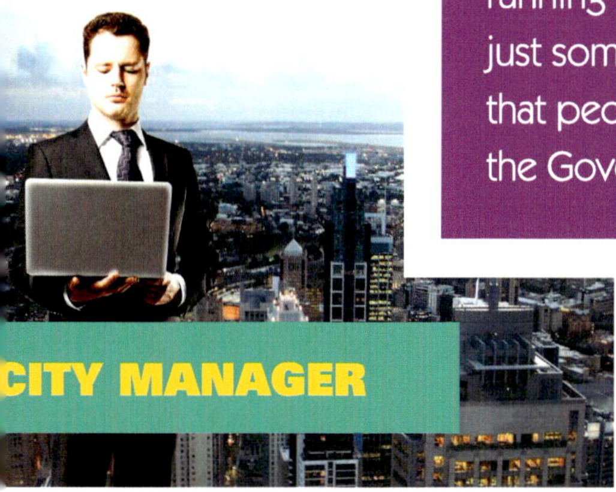

BUILDING INSPECTOR

One thing you'll find in any bustling city is lots of construction—new houses, new schools, even new office skyscrapers. Sometimes old buildings are being replaced. Other times, new construction is making room for more families, businesses, and progress.

The last thing any city needs is poorly constructed buildings. **Building inspectors** work to make sure that buildings are built to last. As the job title suggests, inspectors thoroughly check buildings at several points during the construction process to make sure that everything is being done correctly. They make sure that builders obtain required permits and that all work meets very specific **building codes**.

They double-check the work of skilled craftspeople, too. After all, it takes a team to build a solid structure. Inspectors check on every aspect of the construction, including plumbing, electrical, ventilation, and framing. Nothing is left to chance since people and property are at risk if things are not right.

The only way to know if others are doing their work correctly is to know how to do the work yourself. That's why building inspectors must know a lot about construction to do their jobs. Construction experience is the number one requirement for building inspectors. They work for city or county governments and must pass certification and licensing tests to qualify to do each type of inspection.

Check It Out!

See how skyscrapers are built at

- http://bit.ly/Skyscraper1
- http://bit.ly/Skyscraper2
- http://bit.ly/Skyscraper3

Start Now!

- Talk to your parents about volunteering to help Habitat for Humanity build a home for a family in need.
- Make a checklist of things that need repair around your house or your room.
- Pay attention to construction projects you see around town.

CITY MANAGER

A **city manager** is like the chief executive officer (or CEO) of a city. While a mayor is responsible for setting policy and being the "voice" of a city, the city manager keeps a city running on a day-to-day basis. Mayors are elected by voters, but city managers are appointed by city councils.

Two of a city manager's main jobs involve **budgets** and **staff**. Cities offer many services to their residents, and there is usually a department in charge of providing each type of service. This includes parks and recreation, fire, police, water, and transportation departments. Depending on the size of the city, each department can be rather large. The city manager is usually the boss of the heads of these departments. It is up to the city manager to make sure that citizens get the services they need.

City managers work with each department head to determine how much money is needed to provide each service. They come up with budgets and keep careful watch on how money is spent. They also serve as advisor to the mayor and city council.

City managers have an important job. They have to keep lots of people and departments happy with the decisions they make while always acting in the best interests of the city.

Check It Out!

Go online to find information about your city government. Simply type in the name of your city plus the word "government" to find the correct Web site.

Start Now!

- Make a brochure describing the types of services your city government offers.
- Visit your local city hall to see your city government in action.
- Sign up to learn something new at one of your city's parks or recreation centers.

FIRST RESPONDER

They run into bad situations that cause other people to run away. They put their own safety at risk to keep the rest of us safe. They rescue us from fires and accidents and provide emergency medical treatment when we are hurt or sick. They enforce our laws and protect our property.

They go out of their way to protect us when criminals, **natural disasters**, and other dangers would do us harm.

Who are they?

They are **first responders**. They are the police officers, firefighters, paramedics, and other everyday heroes who make our world a safer place.

They are also city employees who are hired to come to the rescue in all types of emergency situations. Their day-to-day job responsibilities are different, but all types of responders must have at least a high school diploma, be in tip-top physical shape, and go through a detailed application process. Some cities require applicants to have a two-year college degree in a subject like criminal justice. Those chosen to serve must successfully complete challenging training programs. Cities want the best and the brightest wearing their first responder uniforms!

Check It Out!

Talk to your family about making an emergency plan using resources at

https://www.ready.gov/kids

Start Now!

- The next time you see a police officer or firefighter, thank them for keeping your city safe.
- Take a field trip to visit your local fire or police department.
- Sign up to take a first aid or CPR class at your local recreation center.
- Find out if your school participates in law enforcement exploring clubs (www.exploring.org).

INTELLIGENCE ANALYST

Let's start with some definitions. *Intelligence*, in this sense, involves information about what is happening or is going to happen, especially when obtained by spying. To analyze something means to examine something carefully in order to understand what it means.

So, an **intelligence analyst** is someone who pieces together information from a variety of sources in order to understand possible threats and prevent attacks from enemies of our national security.

Intelligence analysts work for all branches of the military. They also work for federal agencies like the **Federal Bureau of Investigation** (FBI), the **Central Intelligence Agency** (CIA), and the **National Security Agency** (NSA). It sounds a bit like alphabet soup, but together these agencies are responsible for keeping America safe from terrorist attacks and other threats. They work with public (available for anyone to see) and classified (considered secret by the government) information.

Some intelligence agencies focus on information gathered from within our own country, while others specialize in data from foreign countries. Those who specialize in other countries must be fluent in that country's native language. So, yes, intelligence analysts tend to be rather intelligent people. They must have a college degree and be skilled in using technology.

Check It Out!

Gather intelligence with the CIA at

- https://www.cia.gov/kids-page/games

Start Now!

- Use the Internet to gather news about the same event from several different sources. Compare the facts presented by each source and highlight any differences.
- Make a poster sharing tips on how to tell fake news from real news.
- Ask a friend or family member to write a secret message using a code and see if you can crack it.

LEGISLATOR

A **legislator** is someone who has been elected to serve in a state or national legislature. To understand what a legislator does, it helps to go back to the word's original Latin meaning. The word *legis*, law. *Lator* means maker or proposer. Put the two together, and a legislator is someone who makes or proposes laws. A legislature is a place where laws are made.

One of the most famous places where legislators come together to make laws is the U.S. Congress. One hundred senators and 435 representatives meet in a building called the U.S. Capitol in Washington, D.C., to make the laws of the land. Each of the 50 United States also has its own legislature that meets in each state's **capital**.

Before a legislator can make laws, he or she must first be elected. That means legislators are also **politicians**. They must **campaign** for the position they seek and convince enough people to vote for them before they can become a legislator. Legislators are elected to serve for a specific period of time, which is usually two or four years.

People who are elected to serve in legislatures come from all walks of life. They tend to be well-educated and successful in other types of work before they run for office. They must be good communicators and able to speak in front of large groups of people. The legislators who get elected—and reelected—have good ideas about what kinds of laws a state or nation needs.

Check It Out!

Use the Internet to find out more about your state's legislature. Type the name of your state plus the words "state legislature" to find the latest news.

Start Now!

- Pop quiz! What are the three branches of government? Go online to find out.
- Make a chart to describe the differences between the two main political parties in the United States: Democrat and Republican.
- Volunteer to help a friend campaign for a position on the student government. Better yet, run for office yourself!

MILITARY SERVICEPERSON

Army! Air Force! Coast Guard! Marines! Navy! These are the five branches of the U.S. military, and they all have distinct missions. **Enlisted personnel** and officers in each of these branches work together to protect our country and defend its interests in other places.

The Air Force provides air and space power by flying planes, helicopters, and satellites. The Army is the biggest land power. In times of conflict, it moves into an area, secures it, and creates order and values before it leaves. The Coast Guard performs rescues, law enforcement, and drug prevention on waterways within the country. The Marines are known as a rapid-reaction force. They are trained to fight by sea and land and usually are the first "boots on the ground." This means they are often the first to arrive in a ground battle. The Navy secures and protects the oceans around the world to create peace and stability. It's their job to make the seas safe for travel and trade.

Once a **military serviceperson** decides which branch to join, he or she can talk to a military recruiter about enlisting. Recruits must make it through a tough **boot camp** before being assigned to duty.

Military officers are trained at one of the military academies: the U.S. Military Academy at West Point, the Air Force Academy, or the U.S. Naval Academy. Or they complete a ROTC (**Reserve Officers' Training Corps**) program at the college where they are earning their degree.

Check It Out!

Explore the five branches of military service at

- http://www.af.mil
- http://www.army.mil
- http://www.marines.mil
- http://www.uscg.mil
- http://www.navy.mil

Start Now!

- Practice saluting like a soldier. For instructions, go to http://www.wikihow.com/Salute-Like-a-Soldier.
- Talk to relatives or family friends about their military service.
- Write a brief essay explaining which branch of military service you like best.

SCIENTIST

Surprise! Did you know that local, state, and national governments employ all kinds of **scientists**? It's true! Scientists work for a wide variety of agencies and departments doing research, making discoveries, and even solving crimes.

Scientists work for the federal government in the Agriculture, Energy, Defense, and other departments. They also work for agencies like the FBI and programs like the National Aeronautics and Space Administration (NASA). They work for state and local governments at parks, museums, and crime laboratories. Pretty much anything you can imagine doing as a scientist can be done as a government employee.

Just like scientists who work at universities and big companies, government scientists must have strong educational backgrounds in their specific types of science. Getting a four-year college degree is often just the beginning as scientists advance in their careers. There are opportunities for scientists who study anything from the skies to animal life to cells—and everything in between.

Name a branch of science and you are sure to find a way that it would be used in government. **Chemists** and **astronomers** apply the physical sciences. Earth scientists work in fields like **meteorology** and **oceanography**. **Biologists** and **botanists** find opportunities to use life sciences in amazing ways.

Check It Out!

Experiment with science information online at

- https://wonderville.org
- http://kids.nationalgeographic.com
- http://discoverykids.com

Start Now!

- Take as many science classes as you can.
- Visit local science and natural history museums.
- Find out if your school offers any STEM clubs or competitions and get involved!

SPECIAL AGENT

Criminals should beware when a **special agent** is on their case! Special agents are detectives or criminal investigators who work for a government agency like the FBI, the Drug Enforcement Agency, or Homeland Security. As federal agents, they investigate serious crimes like kidnapping, bank robbery, cybercrime, drug trafficking, and terrorism.

Special agents also investigate what is known as white-collar crimes. These are crimes that involve money, such as bribery, fraud, and extortion. These types of crimes don't usually involve violence, but they can cause a lot of damage to people, businesses, and governments.

In case you are wondering, the people behind crimes that special agents investigate are in big trouble. Investigations can involve gathering evidence, listening in on a suspect's phone conversations or computer activity, and other detective skills. In some cases, special agents go undercover inside a criminal organization to find out what is going on and catch criminals in the act.

Only the very best candidates get chosen to become special agents. Along with successful law enforcement or military experience, special agents must have a college degree. Being able to speak a foreign language fluently is a desirable skill. Since special agents often deal with dangerous criminals, they must also know how to use guns.

Check It Out!

Learn more about what the FBI does at

- https://archives.fbi.gov/archives/fun-games/kids
- https://sos.fbi.gov

Start Now!

- See if you can solve some online mysteries at http://kids.mysterynet.com.
- Get involved in your school's safety patrol program.
- Volunteer to teach younger students about cybersafety.

Actuarial assistant • Administrative service manager • Adoption services manager • Airport operations manager • Bank examiner • Bank Secrecy Act anti-money laundering officer • Building code administrator • **BUILDING INSPECTOR** • Business manager • Canine (K9) enforcement officer • Case manager • Children's services supervisor • Circuit court clerk • City clerk • **CITY MANAGER** • City planner • City recorder • City tax auditor • Communications director • Community Reinvestment Act officer • Compliance manager • Coroner • Court clerk • Credit union examiner • Crime scene investigator • Criminologist • Customs

WoW Big List

Take a look at some of the different kinds of jobs people do in Government pathway. **WoW!**

Some of these job titles will be familiar to you. Others will be so unfamiliar that you will scratch your head and say "huh?"

and border patrol officer • Customs inspector • Customs port director • Data analyst • Detective • Director of child welfare services • Director of operations • Economist • Emergency management director • Emergency preparedness specialist • Emergency service director • Environmental specialist • Equal opportunity representative • Facilities manager • Financial examiner • **FIRST RESPONDER** • Forensic economist • Forensic pathologist • General manager • Global logistics manager • Government affairs officer • Governor • Housing inspector • Import specialist • **INTELLIGENCE ANALYST** • Intelligence officer • International affairs officer • Law clerk • **LEGISLATOR** • License clerk • Mail superintendent • Mayor • Media relations specialist • Medical examiner • Medical legal examiner • Military officer • **MILITARY SERVICEPERSON** • Motor vehicles clerk • Office manager • Operations manager • Political science teacher • Political scientist • Postmaster • President • Project manager • Public affairs specialist • Public information officer • Quality

Find a job title that makes you curious. Type the name of the job into your favorite Internet search engine and find out more about the people who have that job.

1. What do they do?
2. Where do they work?
3. How much training do they need to do this job?

control officer • Regulatory affairs analyst • Regulatory affairs manager • Research analyst • Revenue officer • **SCIENTIST** • Security manager • Social worker • **SPECIAL AGENT** • Statistical clerk • Supply chain manager • Surveyor • Tax collector • Tax compliance officer • Tax examiner • Traffic manager • Transportation director • Urban planner • Vice president • Workforce service representative • Zoning technician

TAKE YOUR PICK

	Put stars next to your 3 favorite career ideas	Put an X next to the career idea you like the least	Put a question mark next to the career idea you want to learn more about
Building inspector			
City manager			
First responder			
Intelligence analyst			
Legislator			
Military serviceperson			
Scientist			
Special agent			

What do you like most about these careers?	What is it about this career that doesn't appeal to you?	What do you want to learn about this career? Where can you find answers?

Which Big Wow List ideas are you curious about?

Please do **NOT** write in this book if it doesn't belong to you. You can download a copy of this activity online at www.brightfuturespress.com/teacher-guides.

EXPLORE SOME MORE

The Government pathway is only one of 16 career pathways that hold exciting options for your future. Take a look at the other 15 to figure out where to start exploring next.

Architecture & Construction

WOULD YOU ENJOY making things with LEGOs™, building a treehouse or birdhouse, or designing the world's best skate park?

CAN YOU IMAGINE someday working at a construction site, a design firm, or a building company?

ARE YOU CURIOUS ABOUT what civil engineers, demolition technicians, heavy-equipment operators, landscape architects, or urban planners do?

Arts & Communication

WOULD YOU ENJOY drawing your own cartoons, using your smartphone to make a movie, or writing articles for the student newspaper?

CAN YOU IMAGINE someday working at a Hollywood movie studio, a publishing company, or a television news station?

ARE YOU CURIOUS ABOUT what actors, bloggers, graphic designers, museum curators, or writers do?

Business & Administration

WOULD YOU ENJOY playing Monopoly, being the boss of your favorite club or team, or starting your own business?

CAN YOU IMAGINE someday working at a big corporate headquarters, government agency, or international business center?

ARE YOU CURIOUS ABOUT what brand managers, chief executive officers, e-commerce analysts, entrepreneurs, or purchasing agents do?

Education & Training

WOULD YOU ENJOY babysitting, teaching your grandparents how to use a computer, or running a summer camp for neighbor kids in your backyard?

CAN YOU IMAGINE someday working at a college counseling center, corporate training center, or school?

ARE YOU CURIOUS ABOUT what animal trainers, coaches, college professors, guidance counselors, or principals do?

Finance

WOULD YOU ENJOY earning and saving money, being the class treasurer, or playing the stock market game?

CAN YOU IMAGINE someday working at an accounting firm, bank, or Wall Street stock exchange?

ARE YOU CURIOUS ABOUT what accountants, bankers, fraud investigators, property managers, or stockbrokers do?

Food & Natural Resources

WOULD YOU ENJOY exploring nature, growing your own garden, or setting up a recycling center at your school?

CAN YOU IMAGINE someday working at a national park, raising crops in a city farm, or studying food in a laboratory?

ARE YOU CURIOUS ABOUT what landscape architects, chefs, food scientists, environmental engineers, or forest rangers do?

Health Sciences

WOULD YOU ENJOY nursing a sick pet back to health, dissecting animals in a science lab, or helping the school coach run a sports clinic?

CAN YOU IMAGINE someday working at a dental office, hospital, or veterinary clinic?

ARE YOU CURIOUS ABOUT what art therapists, doctors, dentists, pharmacists, and veterinarians do?

Hospitality & Tourism

WOULD YOU ENJOY traveling, sightseeing, or meeting people from other countries?

CAN YOU IMAGINE someday working at a convention center, resort, or travel agency?

ARE YOU CURIOUS ABOUT what convention planners, golf pros, tour guides, resort managers, or wedding planners do?

Human Services

WOULD YOU ENJOY showing a new kid around your school, organizing a neighborhood food drive, or being a peer mediator?

CAN YOU IMAGINE someday working at an elder care center, fitness center, or mental health center?

ARE YOU CURIOUS ABOUT what elder care center directors, hairstylists, personal trainers, psychologists, or religious leaders do?

Information Technology

WOULD YOU ENJOY creating your own video game, setting up a Web site, or building your own computer?

CAN YOU IMAGINE someday working at an information technology start-up company, software design firm, or research and development laboratory?

ARE YOU CURIOUS ABOUT what artificial intelligence scientists, big data analysts, computer forensic investigators, software engineers, or video game designers do?

Law & Public Safety

WOULD YOU ENJOY working on the school safety patrol, participating in a mock court trial at school, or coming up with a fire escape plan for your home?

CAN YOU IMAGINE someday working at a cyber security company, fire station, police department, or prison?

ARE YOU CURIOUS ABOUT what animal control officers, coroners, detectives, firefighters, or park rangers do?

Manufacturing

WOULD YOU ENJOY figuring out how things are made, competing in a robot-building contest, or putting model airplanes together?

CAN YOU IMAGINE someday working at a high-tech manufacturing plant, engineering firm, or global logistics company?

ARE YOU CURIOUS ABOUT what chemical engineers, industrial designers, supply chain managers, robotics technologists, or welders do?

Marketing, Sales & Service

WOULD YOU ENJOY keeping up with the latest fashion trends, picking favorite TV commercials during Super Bowl games, or making posters for a favorite school club?

CAN YOU IMAGINE someday working at an advertising agency, corporate marketing department, or retail store?

ARE YOU CURIOUS ABOUT what creative directors, market researchers, media buyers, retail store managers, and social media consultants do?

Science, Technology, Engineering & Mathematics (STEM)

WOULD YOU ENJOY concocting experiments in a science lab, trying out the latest smartphone, or taking advanced math classes?

CAN YOU IMAGINE someday working in a science laboratory, engineering firm, or research and development center?

ARE YOU CURIOUS ABOUT what aeronautical engineers, ecologists, statisticians, oceanographers, or zoologists do?

Transportation

WOULD YOU ENJOY taking pilot or sailing lessons, watching a NASA rocket launch, or helping out in the school carpool lane?

CAN YOU IMAGINE someday working at an airport, mass transit system, or shipping port?

ARE YOU CURIOUS ABOUT what air traffic controllers, flight attendants, logistics planners, surveyors, and traffic engineers do?

MY WoW

I am here.

Name

Grade

School

Who I am.

Make a word collage! Use 5 adjectives to form a picture that describes who you are.

Where I'm going.

The next career pathway I want to explore is

Some things I need to learn first to succeed.

1

2

3

To get here.

Please do **NOT** write in this book if it doesn't belong to you. You can download a copy of this activity online at www.brightfuturespress.com/teacher-guides.

GLOSSARY

astronomers scientists who study the objects in the sky, including planets, galaxies, black holes, and stars

biologists scientists who focus on living organisms, including plants and animals

boot camp a military training camp for new recruits that is known for very strict discipline

botanists scientists who study plants

budgets plans for how a city spends its money

building codes set of rules adopted by a city to govern the construction of buildings

building inspector person who is employed by a city or county to inspect structuresto make sure they meet building code requirements

campaign to hold a series of events designed to bring about a specific result such as an election

capitol building or group of buildings in which a state or national legislature meets

Central Intelligence Agency (CIA) civilian foreign intelligence service of the U.S. government that gathers, processes, and analyzes national security information from around the world

chemists scientists who work with substances and study what they are made of and how they react with each other

city manager person responsible for directing a variety of administrative processes that allow a city to operate

classified declared secret by the government

enlisted personnel men and women who join the military but are not officers

Federal Bureau of Investigation (FBI) federal law enforcement agency that is responsible for gathering intelligence within the United States

first responder person whose job is to respond first in an emergency, such as a police officer, firefighter, or paramedic

fluent able to speak another language easily and well

intelligence analyst person who works for the government to piece together information from a variety of sources in order to measure threats from inside and outside the United States

legislator person who is elected to a legislature to make or change laws for a country or state

meteorology science of the earth's atmosphere, especially in relation to climate and weather

military serviceperson person who serves in a nation's armed forces

National Security Agency (NSA) intelligence agency of the U.S. government that is responsible for making and breaking codes, protecting communication systems for the military and government, and gathering intelligence data by electronic means

natural disasters natural events such as floods, earthquakes, or hurricanes that cause great damage or loss of life

oceanography science of the ocean and the plants and animals that live in it

politicians people who campaign for or hold a position in government

Reserve Officers' Training Corps (ROTC) college-based programs for training officers of the U.S. armed forces

scientist person who is trained and works in science

special agent person who is a criminal investigator or detective for a federal, state, or county government

staff group of people who work for a company, institution, or government

INDEX

*Air Force, 19
Air Force Academy, 19
Architecture & Construction, 5, 27
*Army, 19
Arts & Communication, 5, 27
*Boy Scouts of America, 15
Business Administration, 5, 27
Central Intelligence Agency, 15
*CIA Kids' Zone, 15
*Coast Guard, 19
Democrat, 17
*Discovery Kids, 21
Drug Enforcement Agency, 22
Education & Training, 5, 27
*Exploring, 15
Federal Bureau of Investigation, 15, 22, 23
*FBI, 23
Finance, 5, 28
Food & Natural Resources, 5, 28
Government & Public Administration, 5
Habitat for Humanity, 8
Health Science, 5, 28
Hospitality & Tourism, 5, 28
*HowStuffWorks, 8
Human Resources, 5, 28
Information Technology, 5, 28
*Inventing the World, 8
Law & Public Safety, 5, 29
Manufacturing, 5, 29
*Marines, 19
*Mystery Net, 23
*National Geographic Kids, 21
National Security Agency, 15
*Navy, 19
*PBS Building the Future, 8
*Ready, 13
Republican, 17
ROTC, 19
Science, Technology, Engineering & Mathematics, 5, 29
Transportation, 5, 29
*U.S. Department of Homeland Security, 22
U.S. Military Academy, 19
U.S. Naval Academy, 19
West Point, 19
*WikiHow, 19
*Wonderville, 21

*** Refers to the Web page sources**

About the Author

Diane Lindsey Reeves is the author of lots of children's books. She has written several original PEANUTS stories (published by Regnery Kids and Sourcebooks). She is especially curious about what people do and likes to write books that get kids thinking about all the cool things they can be when they grow up. She lives in Cary, North Carolina, and her favorite thing to do is play with her grandkids—Conrad, Evan, Reid, and Hollis Grace.